United States Government Accountability Office

Report to Congressional Requesters

I0425856

May 2012

ANTIDUMPING AND COUNTERVAILING DUTIES

Management Enhancements Needed to Improve Efforts to Detect and Deter Duty Evasion

GAO

Accountability ★ Integrity ★ Reliability

GAO-12-551

GAO
Accountability * Integrity * Reliability

Highlights

Highlights of GAO-12-551, a report to congressional requesters

May 2012

ANTIDUMPING AND COUNTERVAILING DUTIES

Management Enhancements Needed to Improve Efforts to Detect and Deter Duty Evasion

Why GAO Did This Study

The United States imposes AD/CV duties to remedy unfair foreign trade practices, such as unfairly low prices or subsidies that cause injury to domestic industries. Examples of products subject to AD/CV duties include honey from China and certain steel products from South Korea. Importers that seek to avoid paying appropriate AD/CV duties may employ methods of evasion such as illegally transshipping an import through a third country to disguise its true country of origin or falsifying the value of an import to reduce the amount of duties owed, among others. AD/CV duty evasion can harm U.S. companies and reduces U.S. revenues. CBP, within the Department of Homeland Security, leads efforts to detect and deter AD/CV duty evasion.

GAO was asked to examine (1) how CBP detects and deters AD/CV duty evasion, (2) factors that affect CBP's efforts, and (3) the extent to which CBP tracks and reports on its efforts. To address these objectives, GAO reviewed CBP data and documents; met with government and private sector representatives in Washington, D.C.; and conducted fieldwork at three domestic ports.

What GAO Recommends

To enhance CBP's efforts to address AD/CV duty evasion and facilitate oversight of these efforts, GAO makes several recommendations, including that CBP create a policy and a mechanism for information sharing among ports regarding the use of higher bond amounts and develop and implement a plan to track and report on these efforts. CBP and the Department of Commerce generally concurred with GAO's recommendations.

View GAO-12-551. For more information, contact Alfredo Gomez at (202) 512-4101 or gomezj@gao.gov.

What GAO Found

U.S. Customs and Border Protection (CBP) detects and deters evasion of antidumping and countervailing (AD/CV) duties through a three-part process that involves (1) identifying potential cases of evasion, (2) attempting to verify if evasion is occurring, and (3) taking enforcement action. To identify potential cases of evasion, CBP targets suspicious import activity, analyzes trends in import data, and follows up on allegations from external sources. If CBP identifies a potential case of evasion, it can use various techniques to attempt to verify whether evasion is occurring, such as asking importers for further information, auditing the records of importers suspected of evasion, and inspecting shipments arriving at ports of entry. If CBP is able to verify evasion, its options for taking enforcement action include (1) pursuing the collection of evaded duties, (2) imposing civil penalties, (3) conducting seizures, and (4) referring cases for criminal investigation. For example, between fiscal years 2007 to 2011, CBP assessed civil penalties totaling about $208 million against importers evading AD/CV duties.

Two types of factors affect CBP's efforts to detect and deter AD/CV duty evasion. First, CBP faces several external challenges in attempting to gather conclusive evidence of evasion and take enforcement action against parties evading duties. These challenges include (1) the inherent difficulty of verifying evasion conducted through clandestine means; (2) limited access to evidence of evasion located in foreign countries; (3) the highly specific and sometimes complex nature of products subject to AD/CV duties; (4) the ease of becoming an importer of record, which evaders can exploit; and (5) the limited circumstances under which CBP can seize goods evading AD/CV duties. Second, gaps in information sharing also affect CBP efforts. Although communication between CBP and the Department of Commerce (Commerce) has improved, CBP lacks information from Commerce that would enable it to better plan its workload and help mitigate the administrative burden it faces in processing AD/CV duties—an effort that diminishes its resources available to address evasion. Additionally, CBP has encouraged the use of larger bond amounts to protect AD/CV duty revenue from the risk of evasion, but CBP has neither a policy nor a mechanism in place for a port requiring a larger bond to share this information with other ports in case an importer withdraws its shipment and attempts to make entry at another port to avoid the higher bond amount.

While CBP has made some performance management improvements, it does not systematically track or report key outcome information that CBP leadership and Congress could use to assess and improve CBP's efforts to deter and detect AC/CV duty evasion. First, CBP cannot readily produce key data, such as the number of confirmed cases of evasion, which it could use to better inform and manage its efforts. Second, CBP does not consistently track or report on the outcomes of allegations of evasion it receives from third parties. As GAO reported in March 2011, the Government Performance and Results Modernization Act of 2010 underscores the importance of ensuring that performance information will be both useful and used in decision making. Without improved tracking and reporting, agency leadership, Congress, and industry stakeholders will continue to have little information with which to oversee and evaluate CBP's efforts to detect and deter evasion of AD/CV duties.

_____ United States Government Accountability Office

Contents

Abbreviations

AD	antidumping
CBP	U.S. Customs and Border Protection
CV	countervailing
Commerce	Department of Commerce
ICE	U.S. Immigration and Customs Enforcement
NTAG	National Targeting and Analysis Group
STB	single transaction bond

United States Government Accountability Office
Washington, DC 20548

May 17, 2012

The Honorable Ron Wyden
Chairman, Subcommittee on International Trade, Customs and Global
 Competitiveness
Committee on Finance
United States Senate

The Honorable Olympia Snowe
United States Senate

The United States imposes antidumping and countervailing (AD/CV) duties to remedy unfair foreign trade practices that cause injury to domestic industries. Importers that seek to avoid paying appropriate AD/CV duties may attempt to evade them through methods such as illegally transshipping an import through a third country to disguise its true country of origin or falsifying the value of an import to reduce the amount of duties owed, among others.[1] Evasion of AD/CV duties undermines U.S. AD/CV duty laws—the intent of which is to level the economic playing field for U.S. industry—and deprives the U.S. government of revenues it is due. U.S. Customs and Border Protection (CBP), within the Department of Homeland Security, leads U.S. efforts to detect and deter AD/CV duty evasion. Congress and domestic industries have expressed concern that unscrupulous actors continue to find ways to evade duties, leaving U.S. industry at risk.

In response to your request for a review of CBP's efforts to address AD/CV duty evasion, this report examines (1) how CBP detects and deters evasion, (2) factors that affect CBP's efforts to detect and deter evasion, and (3) the extent to which CBP tracks and reports on its efforts.

To address these objectives, we reviewed a range of documents and data from CBP related to its efforts to detect and deter AD/CV duty evasion, such as annual planning and reporting documents; internal memos and other documents; and data on products subject to AD/CV duties, allegations of evasion from external sources, and enforcement outcomes.

---

[1]In this report, we use the term "evasion" to refer to any activity whereby companies improperly declare goods that are subject to AD/CV duties to avoid payment of such duties.

GAO-12-551 Antidumping and Countervailing Duties

We also met with officials in CBP's Offices of International Trade, Field Operations, and Intelligence and Investigative Liaison; U.S. Immigration and Customs Enforcement (ICE); and the Departments of Commerce (Commerce) and the Treasury, as well as a coalition of U.S. industries affected by AD/CV duty evasion. Additionally, we conducted fieldwork at the ports of Miami, FL; Seattle, WA; and Los Angeles, CA; as well as the National Targeting and Analysis Group for AD/CV duty issues in Plantation, FL. See appendix I for a complete description of our objectives, scope, and methodology.

We conducted this performance audit from June 2011 to May 2012 in accordance with generally accepted government auditing standards. Those standards require that we plan and perform the audit to obtain sufficient, appropriate evidence to provide a reasonable basis for our findings and conclusions based on our audit objectives. We believe that the evidence obtained provides a reasonable basis for our findings and conclusions based on our audit objectives.

Background

The U.S. Import Process

The process for importing products into the United States involves several different private parties, as well as the U.S. government. These private parties include exporters, carriers, and importers, among others. Exporters are companies that sell goods manufactured or produced in foreign countries to the United States. Carriers are companies that transport the goods to the United States. Importers may be companies that purchase the goods from exporters or simply may be responsible for facilitating the importation of the goods.[2] The importer of record is responsible for paying all estimated duties, taxes, and fees on those products when they are brought into the United States.[3] Importers of record are also required to obtain a general bond to secure the payment

---

[2]See 19 U.S.C. § 1484, which identifies persons who have a right to make entry.

[3]19 U.S.C. § 1505.

of their financial obligations.[4] CBP is responsible for, among other things, managing the import process (see fig. 1); collecting the duties, taxes, and fees assessed on those products; and setting the formula for establishing importers' general bond amounts.[5]

Figure 1: Key Steps in the Import Process

Before goods leave the country of origin, the carrier submits documentation to CBP listing all goods on board destined for the United States.

Goods arrive in the United States. CBP authorizes entry of the goods if no legal or regulatory violations are evident.

After CBP authorizes entry of the goods, the importer submits additional documentation to CBP and pays appropriate duties, taxes, and fees.

Sources: GAO analysis of CBP documentation; PhotoDisc and GAO (photos).

[4]In addition to paying estimated duties, taxes, and fees when products enter the country, importers also are generally required to provide a bond to help ensure that the government can recover additional duties, taxes, or fees that may be owed. See 19 C.F.R. §§ 113.62 and 142.4 for CBP bonding requirements. In general, the importer is required to obtain a bond equal to 10 percent of the amount the importer paid in duties, taxes, and fees over the preceding year (or $50,000, whichever is greater). GAO and CBP both have expressed concern that this general bond inadequately protects AD/CV duty revenue. See GAO, *Antidumping and Countervailing Duties: Congress and Agencies Should Take Additional Steps to Reduce Substantial Shortfalls in Duty Collection*, GAO-08-391 (Washington, D.C.: Mar. 26, 2008).

[5]Legal authority over customs revenue functions is vested in the Secretary of the Treasury and, under Treasury Order 165, was delegated to the U.S. Customs Service. In March 2003, the U.S. Customs Service was transferred to the Department of Homeland Security, and authority over customs revenue functions was delegated to the Department of Homeland Security. 68 Fed. Reg. 10777-01 (Mar. 6, 2003).

GAO-12-551 Antidumping and Countervailing Duties

The United States Imposes AD/CV Duties on a Variety of Imported Goods

The United States and many of its trading partners have established laws to remedy the unfair trade practices of other countries and foreign companies that cause injury to domestic industries. U.S. laws authorize the imposition of AD duties on imports that were "dumped" (i.e., sold at less than normal value)[6] and CV duties on imports subsidized by foreign governments.[7] As we reported in March 2008,[8] the U.S. AD/CV duty system is retrospective, in that importers initially pay estimated AD/CV duties at the time of importation, but the final amount of duties, reflecting the actual amount of dumping or subsidization, is not determined until later.[9] Commerce is responsible for calculating the appropriate AD/CV duty rate.[10] CBP is then responsible for collecting the estimated AD/CV duties when goods enter the United States, and subsequently processing the final AD/CV duties (called "liquidation") when instructed by Commerce.[11] Liquidation may result in providing importers with a refund or sending an additional bill.

A wide range of imported goods are subject to AD/CV duties, such as agricultural, chemical, steel, paper, and wooden products. Each set of AD/CV duties—detailed in an AD/CV duty order—is for a type of product from a specified country. The written "scope" of each AD/CV duty order describes the specific type of product that is subject to the duties. The duty order also lists one or more Harmonized Tariff Schedule codes

---

[6]According to Commerce, the "normal value" is generally the price the foreign firm charges for a comparable product sold in its home market. Under certain circumstances, the normal value may also be the price the foreign firm charges in other export markets or the firm's cost of producing the merchandise, taking into account the firms selling, general, and administrative expenses, and profit. If the producer is located in a non-market economy country, normal value is based on producer's factors of production using values in a "surrogate" market economy country.

[7]The legal authority for the imposition of these duties was created by the Tariff Act of 1930, June 17, 1930, c.497, Title VII. AD duties are authorized in 19 U.S.C. § 1673 and CV duties are authorized in 19 U.S.C. §1671.

[8]GAO-08-391.

[9]The process and time frame for determining AD/CV duties is established by law in title 19 of the United States Code, sections 1671 – 1677n.

[10]19 U.S.C. §§ 1671d, 1673d.

[11]19 U.S.C. §§ 1500, 1505.

associated with the product.[12] There are duty orders in place for some types of products from several countries. For example, there are currently AD duty orders on frozen warmwater shrimp from five countries—Brazil, China, India, Thailand, and Vietnam. For some other types of products, there is a duty order in place on only one country, such as saccharin from China. As of March 2012, there were 283 AD/CV duty orders in effect, with more duty orders on products from China than from any other country (see table 1).[13]

Table 1: Top 5 Countries with Most U.S. AD/CV Duty Orders in Place, as of March 2012

Country	Number of U.S. AD/CV duty orders in place	Examples of product types subject to AD/CV duties
China	114	Honey, saccharin, frozen warmwater shrimp, steel wire hangers
India	23	Mushrooms, matchbooks, frozen warmwater shrimp
Taiwan	16	Steel pipes, ribbons, plastic bags
South Korea	14	Steel pipes, steel plates, diamond sawblades
Japan	13	Steel bars, steel plates, cement

Source: GAO analysis of Commerce data.

---

[12]The Harmonized Tariff Schedule of the United States is the primary resource used by CBP for determining tariff classification for goods imported into the United States. It classifies a good by assigning a 10-digit tariff classification number, based on such things as its name and use, providing CBP detailed information to identify items entering the United States. While tariff codes are used for convenience and customs purposes, the written description of an order is dispositive when determining which merchandise should be subject to AD/CV duties.

[13]These 283 AD/CV duty orders include 234 AD duty orders and 49 CV duty orders.

Evasion of AD/CV Duties

Importers that seek to avoid paying appropriate AD/CV duties may attempt to evade them by using a variety of techniques. These techniques include illegal transshipment to disguise a product's true country of origin, undervaluation to falsify the price of an import to reduce the amount of AD/CV duties owed, and misclassification of merchandise such that it falls outside the scope of an AD/CV duty order, among others (see fig. 2).[14] According to CBP, importers sometimes use more than one evasion method at a time to further disguise the fact that they are importing goods subject to AD/CV duties. Because the techniques used to evade AD/CV duties are clandestine, the amount of revenue lost as a result is unknown.

---

[14]Transshipment is the movement of goods from a country of origin to a country of ultimate destination through an intermediate country. According to CBP, transshipment is legal and commonly used in the ordinary course of business. However, transshipment of merchandise for the purpose of circumventing trade laws—including AD/CV duty laws—is illegal.

Figure 2: Methods Commonly Used to Evade AD/CV Duties

Illegal Transshipment

Disguising a shipment's true country of origin by routing it through an intermediate country not subject to AD/CV duties. This may involve adding false markings and packaging to mimic legitimate production in other countries.

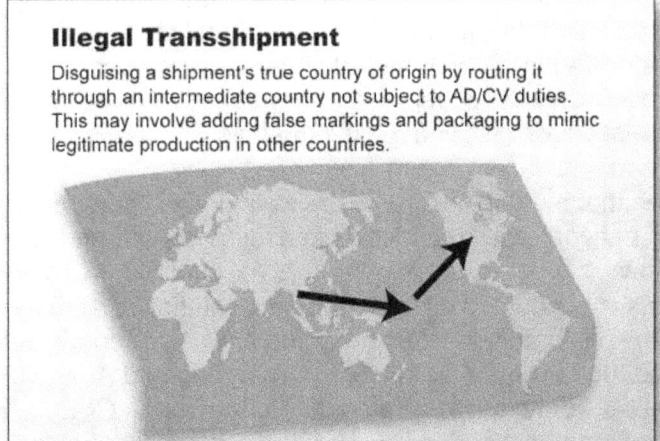

Undervaluation

Falsifying the price of an import to reduce the amount of AD/CV duties assessed.

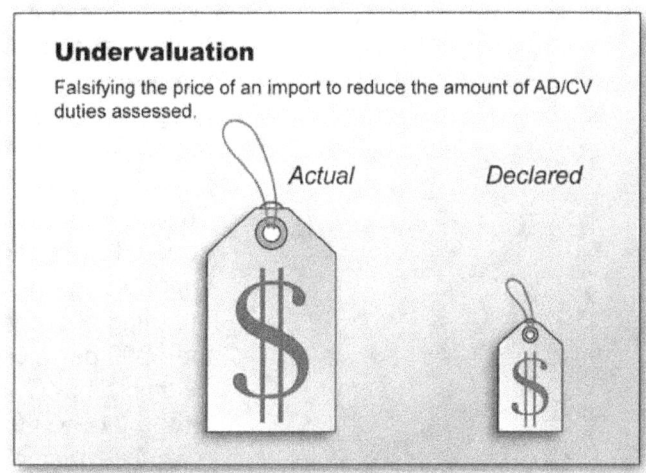

Misclassification

Falsely describing merchandise so that it falls outside the scope of an AD/CV duty order.

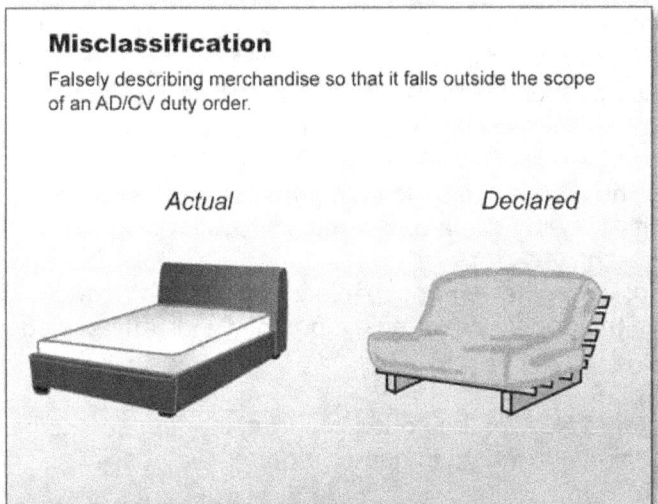

Smuggling

Failing to declare goods on entry documents in order to avoid paying AD/CV duties.

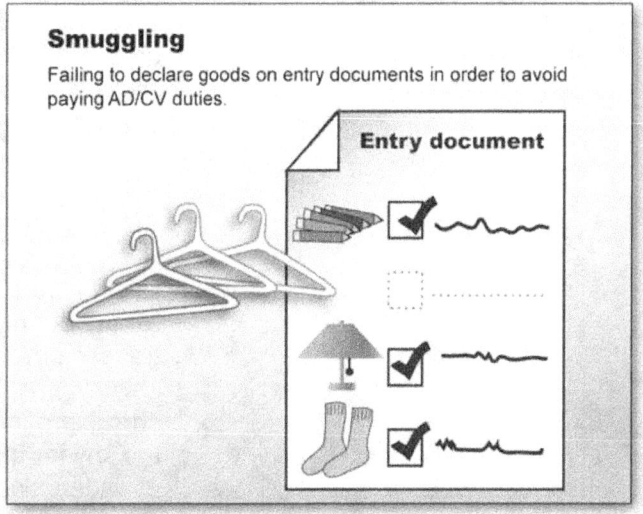

Sources: GAO analysis of CBP documentation; Map Resources (map).

CBP Uses a Three-Part Process to Detect and Deter AD/CV Duty Evasion

CBP detects and deters AD/CV duty evasion through a three-part process that involves (1) identifying potential cases of evasion, (2) attempting to verify if evasion is occurring, and (3) taking enforcement action.

CBP begins its detection of AD/CV duty evasion by identifying potential instances of evasion, using two primary sources of information: import data and allegations from external sources. Import data is generated from the documents submitted by importers as part of the import process. Allegations are collected electronically through e-Allegations, an online system created by CBP in 2008. CBP also collects allegations via other means (such as telephone and e-mail, among others) and stores them in the e-Allegations system. As of September 2011, there were almost 400 allegations related to AD/CV duty evasion in the e-Allegations system, mostly from sources associated with affected industries.[15]

To look for anomalies that may be indicators of evasion, CBP personnel at both the local and national levels conduct targeting, analyze trends in import data, and follow up on allegations from external sources.[16] Local targeting and analysis is conducted by CBP personnel stationed at more than 300 ports of entry, while national targeting and analysis is conducted by officials at CBP headquarters and its National Targeting and Analysis Group (NTAG) for AD/CV duty issues located in Plantation, FL. CBP officials explained that most of their targeting involves identifying entries filed under the Harmonized Tariff Schedule codes associated with a given product that is subject to AD/CV duties and then examining the import documentation for those entries for anomalies that may suggest evasion is occurring. Examples of such anomalies in import documents include, but are not limited to

- being filed under the same tariff code as a product that is subject to AD/CV duties but not being declared as subject to such duties,

- listing a country of origin that is not capable of producing the goods (or the quantity of the goods) imported—a potential indicator of illegal transshipment, and

- showing a monetary value for the goods imported that appears to be too low for the quantity or weight of goods imported—a possible sign of undervaluation.

---

[15]CBP received allegations from congressional sources, Commerce, and anonymous parties, among others.

[16]In this report, we use the term "targeting" to refer to the synthesis and use of information from a variety of sources to identify shipments that may be a potential risk for AD/CV duty evasion.

Once CBP identifies a potential instance of evasion, it can use a variety of techniques at different points in the import process to attempt to verify if evasion is occurring. These include, but are not limited to, the following:

- targeting additional shipments made by the importer of record and conducting further data analysis to look for other anomalies that may be evidence of evasion;

- requesting that the importer provide further information, such as product invoices and other documents that can help CBP understand the transactions involved in producing and importing a good and ascertain if evasion occurred;

- sending referrals to ICE to initiate criminal investigations and gather evidence of evasion from foreign countries, such as by visiting production facilities overseas and collecting customs documents from foreign counterparts;

- performing cargo exams to inspect shipments arriving at ports of entry;

- collecting samples of products potentially brought in through evasion and conducting laboratory analysis of these samples to attempt to identify their true country of origin and other technical details that can help CBP determine if the products should be subject to AD/CV duties; and

- auditing importers suspected of evading AD/CV duties by collecting company records (such as purchase orders, shipping documents, and payment records) and examining them for discrepancies.

Figure 3 shows where in the import process CBP typically uses these techniques.

Figure 3: CBP Techniques for Attempting to Verify Evasion at Different Points in the Import Process

Import process

Before goods leave the country of origin, the carrier submits documentation to CBP listing all goods on board destined for the United States.

Goods arrive in the United States. CBP authorizes entry of the goods if no legal or regulatory violations are evident.

After CBP authorizes entry of the goods, the importer submits additional documentation to CBP and pays appropriate duties, taxes, and fees.

CBP techniques to verify evasion

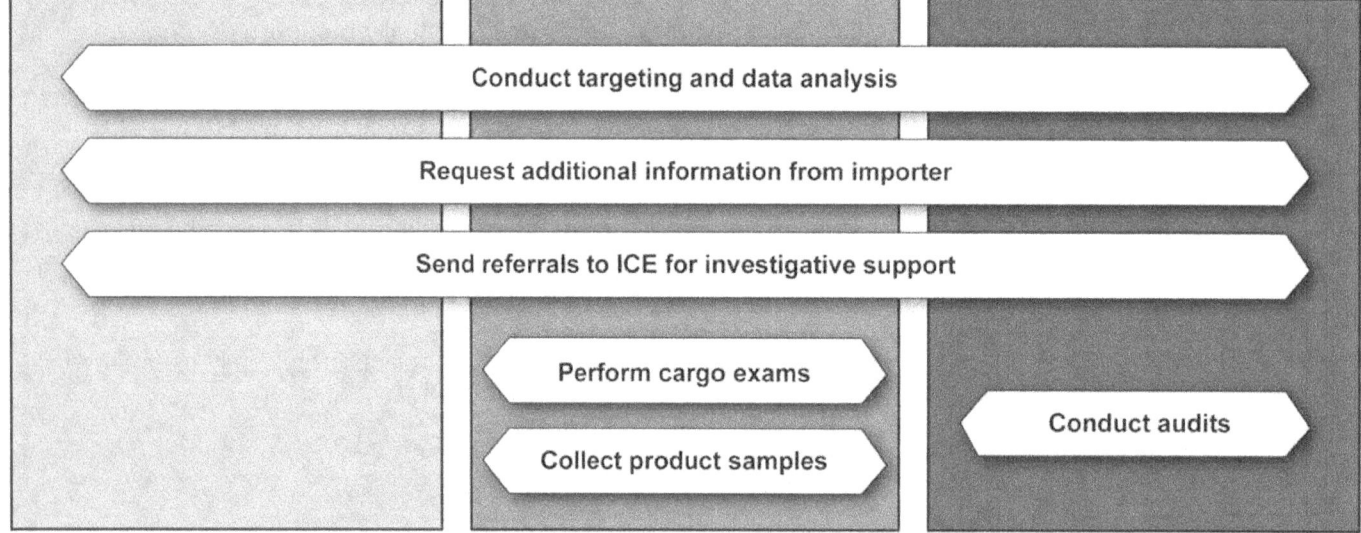

Conduct targeting and data analysis

Request additional information from importer

Send referrals to ICE for investigative support

Perform cargo exams

Collect product samples

Conduct audits

Sources: GAO analysis of CBP documentation; PhotoDisc and GAO (photos).

In cases where CBP is able to verify evasion, its options for taking enforcement action to deter evasion include (1) pursuing the collection of evaded duties, (2) imposing civil penalties, (3) conducting seizures, and (4) referring cases to ICE for criminal investigation. As we discuss later in this report, CBP lacks complete data on the amount of evaded duties it has pursued and collected in cases of evasion. From fiscal years 2007 to 2011, CBP assessed 252 civil penalties totaling about $208 million against 237 importers that evaded AD/CV duties.[17] Over the same period, CBP also made 33 seizures related to AD/CV duty evasion, with a total domestic value of nearly $4 million. In instances where CBP suspects that criminal laws may have been violated, it can refer cases to ICE for criminal investigation.[18] Between fiscal years 2007 and 2011, ICE investigations of AD/CV duty evasion led to 28 criminal arrests, 85 indictments, and 37 criminal convictions.

CBP officials we met with during our review provided examples of how they had recently identified potential cases of evasion, verified that evasion was occurring, and then taken enforcement action. For instance, officials at one port described an effort they initiated following the imposition of CV duties on wood flooring from China. Through a targeting operation using the tariff code for wood flooring, the officials determined that, since the imposition of CV duties on Chinese wood flooring, only 15 of 165 importers with a history of bringing goods from China into their port under the tariff code for wood flooring had begun properly declaring their shipments as entries subject to AD/CV duties—a potential sign of evasion.[19] Subsequently, by conducting cargo exams on several of the suspected importers, the officials were able to verify that the suspected Chinese goods were, in fact, wood flooring, and therefore should have been declared as subject to AD/CV duties (see fig. 4). At the time of our visit, these officials stated that they had collected over $200,000 in unpaid duties from importers that had attempted to evade the AD/CV duties on

---

[17]Under 19 U.S.C. § 1592, irrespective of whether the United States is deprived of lawful duties, CBP can impose penalties against any person who, through fraud, gross negligence, or negligence, enters merchandise into the United States by a material and false act or a material omission. Alternatively, under 19 U.S.C. § 1595a, CBP can impose penalties against any person who directs, assists, or is in any way concerned in importation contrary to law. Importers can challenge the penalties assessed by petitioning CBP. The $208 million penalty amount cited here does not include penalties CBP imposed under 19 U.S.C. § 1595a (importation contrary to law).

[18]ICE officials told us that they may also initiate investigations on the basis of allegations of evasion received from industry parties.

[19]As discussed later in this report, some products that are subject to AD/CV duties fall under the same tariff codes as other products that are not subject to AD/CV duties. Consequently, the tariff code for an entry may be insufficient for CBP to determine whether or not the entry is subject to AD/CV duties; additional information may be needed.

wood flooring and were also preparing to assess civil penalties on 14 importers.

Figure 4: Boxes of Chinese Wood Flooring Brought into the United States through Evasion

At another port we visited, CBP officials described a case that began with an anonymous fax alleging evasion of the AD duties on steel nails from China. After reviewing import data, the officials were able to confirm that the importer named in the allegation had brought an entry of steel nails into their port and that the importer's broker had filed the entry as not subject to AD duties. Because the AD duty order on steel nails from China provides an exemption for roofing nails, the port officials then sent a formal request for information to the importer to ask for a sample of the steel nails imported, which the importer provided.[20] The port officials sent the sample to a CBP laboratory to determine if the nails provided were roofing nails or not. After the laboratory determined that the sample nails

---

[20]Port officials describing this case stated that since they requested a sample after the product had already made entry, the importer could have easily provided a fake sample instead of what was actually imported, but did not do so.

GAO-12-551 Antidumping and Countervailing Duties

were not roofing nails, the port officials concluded that the steel nails were subject to the AD duty order and, consequently, should have been declared as such. The officials subsequently told us that this would result in a penalty against the importer and that 34 additional entries by the importer at six ports were also under review for evasion.

External Obstacles and Gaps in Information Sharing Hamper CBP Efforts to Address Evasion

Two types of factors affect CBP's efforts to detect and deter AD/CV duty evasion. First, CBP faces several external challenges in attempting to gather conclusive evidence of evasion and deter parties from evading duties. Second, although interagency communication has improved, and CBP has encouraged the use of higher bonding requirements to protect revenue, gaps in information sharing with Commerce and within CBP may limit the effectiveness of these initiatives.

CBP Faces Challenges Mostly Beyond Its Control in Proving Evasion Has Occurred and Taking Deterrent Action

Several challenges mostly outside of CBP's control impede its efforts to prove that evasion has occurred and deter parties from evading AD/CV duties. These challenges include (1) the inherent difficulty of verifying evasion conducted through clandestine means; (2) limited access to evidence of evasion located in foreign countries; (3) the highly specific and sometimes complex nature of products subject to AD/CV duties; (4) the ease of becoming an importer of record, which evaders can exploit; and (5) the limited circumstances under which CBP can seize goods brought in through evasion.

Verifying Evasion of AD/CV Duties Is Inherently Difficult and Time-Consuming

CBP officials we met with stated that verifying evasion of AD/CV duties is one of the agency's most challenging and time-consuming trade enforcement responsibilities. As these officials emphasized, proving that evasion is occurring is a key precondition for taking enforcement action against importers evading AD/CV duties. However, because AD/CV duty evasion is inherently deceptive and clandestine in nature, it can be extremely difficult for CBP to gather conclusive evidence to prove that evasion is occurring. According to CBP, not only can different methods of evasion be employed at once—often involving the collusion of several parties, including the manufacturer, shippers, and importer— but entities engaging in evasion are using increasingly complex schemes. In particular, CBP officials identified the growing use of illegal transshipment as a key concern, noting that the Internet has made it very easy for importers to find companies willing to transship goods subject to AD/CV duties through third countries to mask the goods' true country of origin. Because such schemes often involve adding false markings and packaging designed to mimic legitimate production in other countries, it can be very difficult for CBP to determine a product's country of origin through visual inspection or through reviews of shipping documents. Undervaluation can be similarly difficult to prove, according to CBP, especially if the producer and importer collude to create false values.

In addition to being inherently difficult, verifying evasion of AD/CV duties can also be very time-consuming. According to CBP, it can easily take over a year or more to collect the evidence needed to verify a potential case of evasion. For example, CBP's ability to target additional shipments from an importer suspected of evading duties hinges on whether or not importation is ongoing. However, CBP documentation notes that shipments of some goods may be seasonal in nature, resulting in months of inactivity until the next shipment can be targeted. Additionally, in cases where CBP requests additional information from the importer, the importer has 30 days in which to respond to the request, but CBP can extend the deadline in additional 30-day increments if the importer fails to respond or needs more time to gather the required information. Similarly, according to CBP, it typically takes up to 30 days to conduct a laboratory analysis of a product sample, but it can take up to 120 days if, for instance, new analytical methods need to be developed. CBP officials stated that their audits of importers suspected of evading AD/CV duties are also time-consuming in nature, taking nearly 8 months to complete on average. Given these timelines— and the fact that CBP may need to use several such verification techniques to successfully prove a single case of evasion—the process of proving evasion may become quite lengthy.

Limited Access to Evidence of Evasion Located in Foreign Countries Hampers Efforts to Prove Evasion

According to CBP and ICE officials, they have limited access to evidence located in foreign countries that can be vital to proving that evasion has occurred, particularly in cases of illegal transshipment. These officials explained that collecting customs documents from foreign counterparts or gaining access to facilities in a foreign country listed as the country of origin for a suspicious entry can help them prove that the goods in question originated elsewhere. For example, ICE officials investigating a case concerning Chinese honey suspected of being illegally transshipped through Thailand helped determine that evasion occurred, in part by visiting the sites in Thailand where the honey was allegedly produced and determining that the facilities were not honey manufacturing plants (see fig. 5). Similarly, CBP laboratory scientists explained that their ability to use chemical analysis to determine whether an importer falsely declared a good's country of origin is contingent on gathering reference samples from as many countries as possible for comparison purposes.

Figure 5: Facility in Thailand Falsely Described as Honey Manufacturing Plant

Source: ICE.

To collect information located outside of U.S. jurisdiction, CBP and ICE need to obtain the permission of host nation governments. However, both CBP and ICE explained that the level of host nation cooperation varies. According to ICE, even when the United States has bilateral agreements in place to share customs information, the extent of information shared by foreign counterparts varies by country. For example, ICE officials stated that although most of their investigations of evasion involve goods from China—with which the United States has a customs cooperation agreement in place—they have never received permission to visit facilities in China as part of their investigations. Similarly, according to ICE officials, although the United States has bilateral agreements with several countries that are thought to be common transshipment points—such as Indonesia, India, and the Philippines—ICE's ability to visit these and other countries during the course of investigations depends on factors such as each country's political climate, the nature of its bilateral relationship with the United States, and the extent to which the host nation government has ties to the company or industry under investigation. CBP laboratory scientists have also had mixed results in gaining access overseas. They noted that the Indonesian government recently allowed them access to collect samples of shrimp from Indonesian producers. However, the Malaysian government initially gave them approval to visit honey and shrimp producers in their country but ultimately rescinded its approval without explanation. CBP officials also noted that although the U.S. free trade agreement with Singapore—another country thought to be a common transshipment point—allows for cooperation on customs issues, the agreement explicitly excludes matters related to AD/CV duties.

Specificity and Complexity of Products Subject to AD/CV Duties Complicate CBP Efforts to Identify Evasion

According to CBP officials, the highly specific and complex nature of some products subject to AD/CV duties can make it extremely difficult to identify evasion. As noted earlier, most of CBP's targeting for potential evasion involves examining entries that have the same Harmonized Tariff Schedule codes as products subject to AD/CV duties in order to look for any not filed as subject to AD/CV duties. For example, to target potential evasion of the AD duties on saccharin from China, CBP can examine entries from China that have the tariff code for saccharin and determine if any have been filed as not subject to AD/CV duties. However, in some cases, no unique tariff code exists for the specific products that Commerce investigated and issued a duty order for; rather, these products fall under the same tariff code as a broader category of products that are not subject to AD/CV duties. Consequently, the tariff codes listed on a given entry may be insufficient for CBP to determine if goods imported as part of that shipment are subject to AD/CV duties; additional information may be needed. An example is petroleum wax candles from China, which are subject to AD duties. Because there is no specific tariff code for petroleum wax candles—only one for candles—CBP cannot conclude, absent other evidence, that an entry from China under the tariff code for candles is petroleum wax candles, as it may be another type of candle that is not subject to AD duties. Instead, CBP has to turn to other means of verification to attempt to gather conclusive evidence that the entry is petroleum wax candles and, therefore, subject to AD duties. For example, CBP may decide to ask the importer for additional information, such as product invoices containing further details on the type of candles imported. CBP may also target additional shipments of candles and potentially collect a sample for laboratory analysis. However, as described earlier, each of these steps would take additional time, lengthening the verification process.

According to CBP officials, the complex nature of some products covered by AD/CV duty orders can also make it difficult for CBP personnel to visually identify the products during cargo exams. For instance, CBP officials stated that AD/CV duty orders on steel typically cover steel products with a certain chemical composition—an aspect that cannot be determined through visual inspection. Another example is the AD/CV duty order on honey, which applies not only to natural honey and flavored honey, but also to honey blends that contain more than 50 percent natural honey by weight—a characteristic that cannot be ascertained by sight alone. In such cases, CBP personnel can extract a sample from the shipment and send it for laboratory analysis. However, CBP laboratory scientists stated that chemical analysis does not always return a definitive judgment of whether or not a product sample analyzed should fall within the scope of an AD/CV duty order. For example, chemical analysis of a honey blend can return inconclusive results if certain additives are present in the blend. CBP officials stated that CBP cannot take enforcement action without conclusive proof of evasion.

Evaders Can Exploit the Ease of Becoming an Importer of Record, Impeding CBP Efforts to Target and Deter Evasion

Entities engaging in evasion can exploit the ease of becoming an importer of record, impeding CBP's ability to target and take deterrent action against them. As noted earlier, importers of record are responsible for paying all estimated duties, taxes, and fees on products when they are brought into the United States. However, importers seeking to evade AD/CV duties can exploit the ease of becoming an importer of record in several ways. First, according to CBP officials, companies can easily adopt new importer names and identification numbers, making it difficult for CBP to track their importing activity and gather evidence needed to prove that they are engaging in evasion. CBP officials stated that they suspect some importers evading AD/CV duties set up new names and identification numbers in advance to have ready for use in anticipation of CBP targeting efforts. Second, as our prior work has noted, CBP collects a minimal amount of information from companies applying to be importers of record, which evaders can take advantage of to elude CBP efforts to locate and collect revenues from them.[21] For instance, companies are not subject to any credit or background checks before being allowed to import products into the United States. Third, foreign companies and individuals are allowed to import products into the United States, but CBP can have difficulty collecting duties and penalties from foreign importers—especially illegitimate ones—when the importers have no attachable assets in the United States. For example, as of February 2012, CBP had collected about $5 million, or about 2 percent, of the approximately $208 million it assessed in civil penalties between fiscal years 2007 and 2011. CBP attributed its collection difficulties, in part, to challenges experienced in

---

[21]GAO-08-391.

collecting from foreign importers of record.[22] CBP officials stated that, due to this risk of noncollection, a factor they consider when deciding whether or not to impose a penalty against a confirmed evader is whether or not it has assets in the United States.

As we have previously reported, CBP or Congress could heighten the requirements for becoming an importer of record; however, such action could lead to unintended consequences.[23] Heightened requirements could include mandatory financial or background checks. However, performing these checks would create a significant new burden on CBP, which would need to conduct or oversee these financial or background checks. Additionally, it is possible that, to ensure fairness, the heightened requirements would be imposed on all importers. Given that the vast majority of importers comply with customs laws and pay their duty liabilities, such a broad approach may not be cost-effective and could potentially restrict trade.

Circumstances under Which CBP Can Seize Shipments Brought in through Evasion Are Limited

CBP is able to seize goods imported through evasion under limited circumstances. CBP officials explained that unlike goods that are illegal to import, such as those violating import safety or intellectual property laws, goods imported through evasion are not necessarily illegal to import. Specifically, according to CBP, although misclassification and undervaluation are commonly used evasion schemes, U.S. trade law limits the seizure of shipments that are misclassified or undervalued.[24] By contrast, CBP is permitted to seize shipments brought in through other forms of evasion, such as through falsifying the country of origin of goods (illegal transshipment) or failing to declare goods on entry documents

---

[22]As our prior work indicates, another factor that can lead the amount of penalties CBP ultimately collects to be lower than the amount initially assessed is successful petition by an importer. See GAO, *Options for Collecting Revenues on Liquidated Entries of Merchandise Evading Antidumping and Countervailing Duties*, GAO-12-131R (Washington, D.C.: Nov. 2, 2011).

[23]GAO-08-391.

[24]Under 19 U.S.C. § 1595a, shipments imported contrary to United States classification or valuation law, where there are no issues as to the admissibility of the merchandise into the Unites States, can only be seized in accordance with 19 U.S.C. § 1592.

(smuggling).[25] Of the 33 seizures CBP made between fiscal years 2007 and 2011, at least 28 were related to false country of origin or smuggling. For instance, CBP officials at one port seized a shipment of plastic bags following a cargo exam that revealed the shipment's country of origin had been falsified. However, as CBP has testified before Congress, entities engaging in evasion often use false markings and packaging that make it very difficult to determine country of origin through visual examination alone, complicating the task of establishing grounds for seizure. Moreover, as noted earlier, verifying evasion is an inherently difficult and time-consuming process. CBP officials stated that, by the time CBP is able to verify an instance of evasion, the associated goods typically have already entered the United States and cannot be seized.

Interagency Communication Has Improved and CBP Has Promoted Use of Higher Bonding Requirements to Protect Revenue, but Weaknesses in Information Sharing Remain

Communication between Commerce and CBP has improved since our 2008 report on AD/CV duties, and CBP has encouraged port officials to use higher bonding requirements to protect AD/CV duty revenue when they suspect incoming shipments of evasion. However, CBP lacks information from Commerce that would enable it to better plan its workload and minimize the burden of the U.S. retrospective system on its efforts to address evasion. Additionally, CBP has neither a policy nor a mechanism in place for a port requiring a higher bond to share this information with other ports in case an importer attempts to "port-shop," i.e., chooses to withdraw its shipment and attempts to make entry at another port in an attempt to avoid the larger bond requirement.

Despite Improved Communication with Commerce, CBP Lacks Information Needed to Mitigate Burden of Retrospective System on Efforts to Address Evasion

CBP officials cited the administrative burden of the U.S. retrospective system as a factor that diminishes the resources they have available for detecting and deterring evasion of AD/CV duties. Under the U.S. retrospective system, importers that properly declare their products as subject to AD/CV duties (i.e., do not evade) pay the estimated amount of duties when products enter the United States, but the final amount of duties owed is not determined until later. The documentation for the entries remains at the ports while CBP awaits liquidation instructions conveying the final duty rate from Commerce. Commerce's review to

---

[25]CBP can also seize goods suspected of evading AD/CV duties if it can prove that the goods violate other laws. For instance, CBP officials at one port we visited stated that they were able to seize shipments of honey suspected of evasion after a sample they sent to the Food and Drug Administration for testing was found to contain a carcinogenic substance, thereby violating import safety law—a legitimate reason for seizure.

determine the final duty rate—a process that culminates with the issuance of liquidation instructions—typically takes up to 18 months to complete and can take months or years longer if litigation is involved.[26] At one port we visited, CBP officials stated that they had approximately 20,000 entries awaiting instructions to liquidate for food-related products alone. At another port, officials showed us the file room where they store entries awaiting liquidation instructions (see fig. 6). Moreover, each of the thousands of entries subject to AD/CV duties must be liquidated through manual data entry, which is resource- and time-intensive and diverts CBP personnel from their efforts to detect and deter evasion.

Figure 6: Unliquidated Entries Subject to AD/CV Duties Stored in File Room at a U.S. Port of Entry

Source: GAO.

Under U.S. law, CBP has 6 months to liquidate entries from the time that it receives notice of the lifting of suspension of liquidation.[27] According to CBP officials, this 6-month deadline can be very difficult to meet,

---

[26]During this review, which is known as an administrative review, Commerce analyzes previous imports to determine the actual level of dumping or subsidization for those imports and calculate the final duty rate.

[27]19 U.S.C. § 1504(d). Liquidation of entries subject to AD/CV duties is suspended until removed by statute or by court order.

especially when a large volume of imports needs to be liquidated.[28] In order to begin liquidating entries, CBP must first receive liquidation instructions from Commerce.

Since our 2008 report, Commerce has taken steps to improve the transmission of its liquidation instructions to CBP. We found in 2008 that, about 80 percent of the time, Commerce failed to send liquidation instructions within its self-imposed deadline of 15 days after the publication of the *Federal Register* notice. Furthermore, we reported that the instructions were sometimes unclear, thereby causing CBP to take extra time to obtain clarification.[29] Consequently, we identified untimely and unclear liquidation instructions from Commerce as an impediment to CBP's ability to liquidate entries. In response to our recommendation to identify opportunities to improve liquidation instructions, Commerce took steps to improve the transmission of liquidation instructions to CBP. For instance, Commerce deployed a system for tracking when it sends liquidation instructions, which according to Commerce, has greatly improved its timeliness. Documentation from Commerce indicates that, in the first half of fiscal year 2012, Commerce sent liquidation instructions on a timely basis more than 90 percent of the time. In addition, Commerce and CBP jointly established a mechanism for CBP port personnel to submit questions directly to Commerce regarding liquidation issues. According to CBP officials, these steps have improved the ability of port personnel to ask Commerce to clarify its liquidation instructions.

Despite these improvements, CBP officials stated that they lack information from Commerce needed to effectively manage their workload. Specifically, although CBP and Commerce both characterized their interagency working relationship as cooperative, CBP officials stated that Commerce does not provide them with advance notice on a regular basis before issuing liquidation instructions, impairing their ability to make workload decisions that could help mitigate the impact of the liquidation process on their efforts to detect and deter evasion. Similarly, we testified

---

[28]When CBP is unable to complete the liquidation process within 6 months, an entry is "deemed liquidated," and the entry is liquidated at the rate assessed at the time of entry. This precludes CBP from attempting to collect any supplemental additional duties that might have been owed because of an increase in the AD/CV duty rate. Similarly, it means that CBP does not refund money owed to importers as a result of a decrease in the AD/CV duty rate, absent a proper protest by the importer.

[29]GAO-08-391.

in May 2011 that, without advance notice from Commerce on upcoming liquidation instructions, it can be very difficult for CBP to make workforce planning and staffing decisions. CBP officials at headquarters and at ports we visited stated that liquidation instructions arrive with little warning but need to be acted on immediately due to the 6-month deadline for liquidating entries. They said that this sudden shift in workload diverts key personnel from efforts to address evasion to focus on manually liquidating thousands of entries instead. In the absence of advance notice from Commerce on upcoming liquidation instructions, CBP attempts to roughly estimate where its workload peaks will occur on the basis of the 18-month time frame within which Commerce typically completes liquidation instructions. However, CBP officials stated that no such estimation is possible in cases involving litigation, which are not subject to time frames. According to CBP, cases involving litigation are particularly burdensome because of the considerable length of time it can take to resolve some cases, during which an extremely large number of entries can accumulate at the ports—all of which CBP eventually has to attempt to liquidate within the 6-month deadline. However, Commerce does not currently inform CBP when a court reaches a decision on a case in litigation—information that would enable CBP to conduct some workload planning. According to CBP officials, since CBP is not a party to such cases, it would be helpful if Commerce provided them with some notification once decisions are reached. Commerce officials stated that they do not know when courts will reach decisions on cases in litigation, but said that they could work with CBP to identify opportunities to share information regarding the status of litigation.

In response to a CBP request, Commerce recently provided CBP some information for the first time to help with workload planning. In June 2011, Commerce officials provided their counterparts in CBP headquarters with a list of instructions planned for issuance over the next 6 months. CBP officials at headquarters acknowledged receiving the list from Commerce, stating that, although the list did not address their need to know when courts reach decisions on cases involving litigation, they found it useful for general workload planning purposes. They noted that they would like to receive this type of list from Commerce on a quarterly basis to have more up-to-date information on hand to incorporate into their workload planning decisions. Commerce officials stated that they would be willing to work with CBP to develop a schedule for sharing this list on a regular basis.

CBP Has Encouraged Use of Higher Bonding Requirements to Protect Additional Revenue from Risk of Evasion, but Gaps Exist in Information Sharing

CBP has encouraged the use of higher bonding requirements, called single transaction bonds (STB), to protect AD/CV duty revenue from the risk of evasion; however, it has not ensured that a port requiring an STB shares this information with other ports in case an importer withdraws its shipment and attempts to make entry at another port to avoid the STB. As noted earlier, all importers are required to post a security, usually a general obligation bond, when they import products into the United States.[30] This bond is an insurance policy protecting the U.S. government against revenue loss if an importer defaults on its financial obligations as well as ensuring compliance with the law.[31] However, given CBP's concerns that this general bond inadequately protects AD/CV duty revenue, CBP has encouraged port officials to protect additional revenue by requiring STBs for individual shipments they suspect of evasion.[32] The amount of the STB is generally one to three times the total entered value of the merchandise plus duties, taxes, and fees, depending on the revenue risk. According to CBP officials, STBs serve as additional insurance in cases where CBP has not been able to collect enough evidence before a shipment's arrival to prove that evasion is occurring, but where enough suspicion exists about the shipment to warrant protection of the anticipated AD/CV duty revenue. An importer that is required to obtain an STB can either choose to post the bond in order to enter its shipment, or can opt against obtaining the bond and withdraw its shipment. If an importer decides to post the STB, and CBP later confirms that AD/CV duties are indeed owed, CBP first tries to collect from the importer. However, if CBP is unable to collect from the importer, it can collect significantly more money from the surety (insurance) company that underwrote the STB than it would typically be able to collect from the surety on a general bond, given the larger amount of revenue protected by the STB.

While CBP has encouraged the use of STBs to protect revenue related to imports suspected of AD/CV duty evasion, vulnerabilities exist due to gaps in port-level information sharing. CBP gives each port the discretion

---

[30]19 C.F.R. § 142.4.

[31]19 U.S.C. § 1623. In general, the importer is required to obtain a bond equal to 10 percent of the amount the importer paid in duties, taxes, and fees over the preceding year (or $50,000, whichever is greater).

[32]During our review, CBP was unable to provide data on the number of STBs port officials have required.

to decide when to require an STB. However, CBP has no policy or mechanism in place for ports requiring such a bond to share this information with other ports in case an importer attempts to port-shop, i.e., chooses to withdraw its shipment and attempts to make entry at another port in an attempt to avoid the larger bond requirement. Instead, CBP port officials currently rely on informal e-mail and telephone communication to notify other port officials of importers potentially seeking to port-shop. Officials we met with cited specific instances where this informal approach had been ineffective in notifying other ports of suspected evasion before the importer could enter the goods at another port. For example, CBP officials at one port described a case where an importer that decided against posting an STB at their port was able to make entry in another port before they were able to e-mail a warning about that particular importer to other ports. In another case, an importer succeeded in entering a shipment of furniture in Newark after officials at the initial port of entry on the West Coast failed to notify other ports that the importer had decided to withdraw its entry instead of posting an STB. In both cases, CBP port officials suspected evasion but did not take additional action in time to warn other ports of entry about the potential for port-shopping.

Although CBP is currently formulating policy to guide the use of STBs, the policy may not fully address the risk of port-shopping. In February 2012, CBP officials stated that they were in the process of completing a policy that will further encourage port officials to use STBs and provide them with guidance on circumstances under which the use of STBs is appropriate.[33] Officials stated that the policy will also instruct officials at a port requiring an STB to review any other shipments from the importer in question before releasing them. They added that they had not yet decided whether or not to automatically instruct ports nationwide to conduct the same level of review.

---

[33]Commerce officials stated that they would be willing to assist CBP with this policy.

CBP Has Made Some Performance Management Improvements but Does Not Systematically Track or Report on Its Efforts to Detect and Deter Evasion

While CBP has improved its performance measures for addressing AD/CV duty evasion and enhanced its monitoring of STBs, it does not systematically track or report key outcome information that CBP leadership and Congress could use to assess and improve CBP's efforts to detect and deter AD/CV duty evasion. First, CBP cannot readily produce key data on AD/CV duty evasion, such as the number of confirmed cases of evasion, which it could use to better inform and manage its efforts. Second, CBP does not consistently track or report on the outcomes of allegations of evasion it receives from third parties. As we have previously reported, internal control is a major part of managing an organization and should be generally designed to assure that ongoing monitoring occurs in the course of normal operations.[34] Furthermore, our prior work has noted the need for agencies to consider the differing information needs of various users, such as agency top leadership and Congress. Specifically, as we reported in March 2011, the Government Performance and Results Modernization Act of 2010 underscores the importance of ensuring that performance information will be both useful and used in decision making.[35]

CBP Has Improved Performance Measures and Began Monitoring the Use of STBs

In the past year, CBP has made enhancements in the following two areas to track its efforts related to combating AD/CV duty evasion:

- *CBP has taken steps to improve the performance measures for its efforts to detect and deter AD/CV duty evasion.* CBP told us that in fiscal years 2010 and 2011, a majority of the performance measures for AD/CV duty enforcement either lacked sufficient data or were declared to be "not measurable." For example, CBP considered one measure for fiscal year 2011—"analysis completed and enforcement alternatives concurred"— too broad to collect data and report on, given the large number of CBP offices that conduct analysis and enforcement. In another example, CBP did not provide a response to the fiscal year 2011 performance measure related to the results of cargo exams because, according to CBP officials, cargo exams are conducted at the local level and not tracked, creating a dearth of

---

[34]GAO, *Internal Control: Standards for Internal Control in the Federal Government*, GAO/AIMD-00-21.3.1 (Washington, D.C.: November 1999).

[35]See GAO, *GPRA Modernization Act Provides Opportunities to Help Address Fiscal, Performance, and Management Challenges*, GAO-11-466T (Washington, D.C.: Mar. 16, 2011).

GAO-12-551 Antidumping and Countervailing Duties

reportable data. In addition, CBP was unable to track and assess its efforts over time because its measures were inconsistent from year to year.

By contrast, CBP's fiscal year 2012 action plan includes a new set of performance metrics with measurable targets consistent from fiscal years 2012 through 2017. For example, the performance measure for penalties issued has targets to increase the amount of penalties issued each year by 10 or 15 percent. There are similar measures with targets for increasing the percentage of AD/CV duties collected and the number of audits related to AD/CV duties.

- *CBP is working to improve its ability to track and report on the use of STBs.* In June 2011, after finding that CBP could not determine the total number of STBs used at the ports, the Department of Homeland Security Inspector General recommended that CBP appoint a centralized office responsible for reporting STB-related activities and monitoring results.[36] The Inspector General's report also recommended that CBP automate the STB process to provide enhanced tracking ability. CBP concurred with these recommendations, stating that it had begun the process of centralizing STB-related roles and responsibilities and developing a system to automate the STB process. Moreover, one of the new measures in the fiscal year 2012 action plan tracks the number of STBs used for AD/CV duty evasion.

CBP Lacks Key Data to Effectively Manage Its Efforts to Detect and Deter Evasion

While CBP has reported anecdotes about its successes in addressing AD/CV duty evasion and collects some statistics on its efforts, it lacks key data that it could use to assess and improve its management practices and that could enhance congressional oversight. Over the past year, CBP has publicly reported anecdotes of successful efforts to detect and deter AD/CV duty evasion. For example, in testimony before Congress in May 2011, the Assistant Commissioner for CBP's Office of International Trade described five recent cases where CBP and ICE uncovered instances of evasion and penalized those responsible. Similarly, in a report to Congress on fiscal year 2010 efforts to enforce AD/CV duties, CBP cited eight cases that led to enforcement action against parties engaging in evasion. CBP has also produced publicly available videos illustrating a

---

[36]Department of Homeland Security Office of Inspector General, *Efficacy of Customs and Border Protection's Bonding Process*, OIG-11-92 (Washington, D.C.: June 27, 2011).

successful case where CBP worked with ICE to arrest and convict an importer who evaded the AD/CV duties on wire hangers.

CBP collects some statistics on its efforts to detect and deter AD/CV duty evasion but lacks other key data on these efforts. For example, CBP provided us with statistics on civil penalties and seizures related to AD/CV duty evasion. However, CBP lacks data on

- the total number of confirmed cases of AD/CV duty evasion;

- the total amount of duties assessed and collected for confirmed cases of evasion;

- the country of origin, product type, and method of evasion for each confirmed case of evasion; and

- the number of confirmed cases of evasion involving a foreign importer of record.

CBP attributed this lack of data to the absence of a policy requiring officials to record confirmed cases of AD/CV duty evasion. CBP officials explained that although CBP has a database in which instances of evasion could be recorded, current policy does not require officials to record such instances. Consequently, CBP cannot conduct a simple data query to identify all confirmed cases of evasion. Without the ability to identify cases of evasion, CBP cannot easily access other related data on AD/CV evasion that could help improve management decisions and oversight. For example, CBP is currently unable to produce data on the total amount of duties assessed and collected for confirmed cases of evasion—figures that would provide CBP leadership and Congress visibility over some of the results of CBP's efforts to address evasion. Similarly, comprehensive data on the country of origin, product type, and method of evasion for each confirmed case of evasion could potentially help CBP identify trends and shifts in evasive activity and make adjustments accordingly.

CBP also lacks complete data on the country of origin and product type associated with the 252 civil penalties it imposed for AD/CV duty evasion between fiscal years 2007 and 2011 (see fig. 7). CBP attributed these missing data items to CBP personnel not recording them in CBP's automated system for tracking penalties. Due to these missing data items, CBP lacks a complete picture of the countries and commodities involved in its penalty cases—information it could use to guide and improve its efforts. For example, CBP could identify which types of commodities have led to penalties most often and decide whether or not to focus more resources and detection efforts on those types of commodities.

Figure 7: Missing Data on Civil Penalties CBP Imposed between Fiscal Years 2007 and 2011 for AD/CV Duty Evasion, as of February 2012

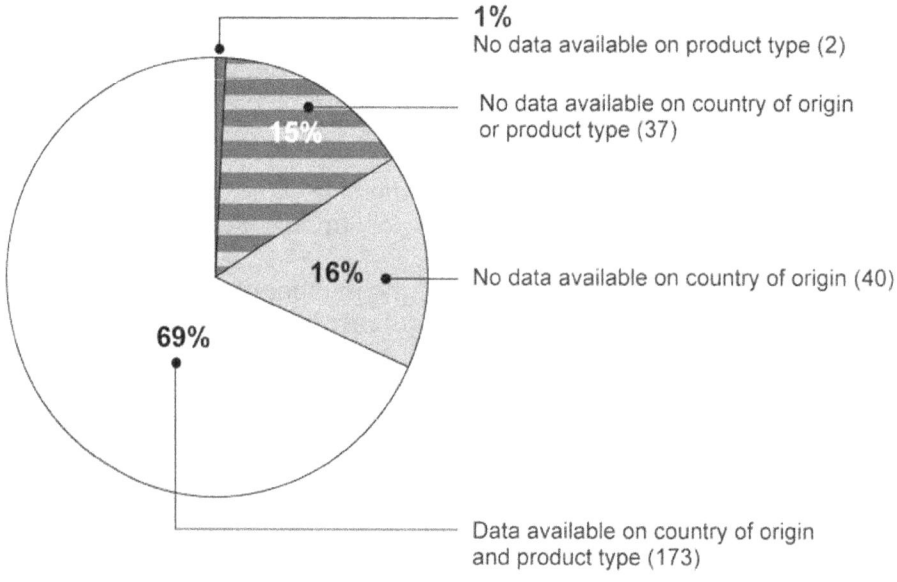

1%
No data available on product type (2)

No data available on country of origin or product type (37)

No data available on country of origin (40)

Data available on country of origin and product type (173)

Source: GAO analysis of CBP data.

Note: Percentages do not add to 100 due to rounding.

CBP Does Not Consistently Track or Report Outcomes of Allegations of Evasion

According to CBP officials, CBP addresses all allegations of AD/CV duty evasion it receives, including e-Allegations received online, but it does not routinely track or report on the outcomes of these allegations. As a result, Congress and industry stakeholders lack information about the outcomes of the allegations, which both parties have cited as a cause of concern. Data from CBP indicate that it generally assigns allegations to its national targeting staff for AD/CV duty issues (i.e., the NTAG) within 2 days of receipt. The NTAG then assesses the validity of the allegation using targeting and other analytical tools. If the NTAG determines that the allegation may be valid, it will typically refer the allegation to the appropriate port or to ICE for further investigation and possible enforcement action. As of September 2011, CBP had confirmed or referred nearly one-quarter of the approximately 400 allegations it

GAO-12-551 Antidumping and Countervailing Duties

received from 2008 to August 2011. About half could not be validated, and another one-quarter were still under analysis.

Although CBP has stated that it addresses all allegations of AD/CV duty evasion it receives, it has reported little information to date on the outcomes of its efforts to follow up on these allegations. For instance, CBP's report to Congress on AD/CV duty enforcement efforts in fiscal year 2010 mentions that CBP has received hundreds of allegations from the trade community, but the report includes no information on the outcomes of those allegations. In January 2011, in response to a congressional request, CBP produced a spreadsheet of the allegations it had received since June 2008. CBP officials told us that this spreadsheet was created upon request and is not something CBP updates or uses for management or policy purposes. While this document lists certain details, such as the source of each allegation, and identifies allegations of evasion that CBP confirmed as valid, it does not include any information on the associated enforcement outcomes. During the course of our review, CBP provided us with expanded versions of the spreadsheet in response to our request for details on the results of the allegations. However, these expanded versions provide little insight into the results of the allegations. For instance, the most recent version of the spreadsheet that we received, from September 2011, documents the enforcement outcome for only one of the 24 allegations labeled as "allegation confirmed." CBP was also unable to determine if the allegations referred to ports and ICE by the NTAG were subsequently confirmed as valid or resulted in enforcement outcomes.

CBP's limited reporting on the outcomes of allegations is due, in part, to inconsistent, decentralized tracking of such information. CBP officials stated that once the NTAG has referred an allegation to a port or to ICE for further action, CBP considers the allegation to be closed and may or may not follow up to track its outcome. While CBP creates a record within its Commercial Allegation and Reporting System for each allegation it receives, there is no requirement for either the NTAG or the entity receiving the allegation referral to update these records with details on its enforcement outcomes. Instead, port officials and ICE store information on enforcement outcomes in other data systems that are not linked to the Commercial Allegation and Reporting System. CBP officials at headquarters told us that aggregating data from these various systems to link allegations with their associated outcomes would be difficult and time-consuming. Additionally, according to ICE, it does not specifically track cases generated as a result of allegations referred by CBP. Consequently, since ICE cannot identify which of its cases involve allegations referred from CBP, it also cannot identify the associated outcomes.

An additional cause of CBP's limited reporting on the outcomes of allegations is legal restrictions on the types of information it can share. During our review, we met with representatives of a coalition of domestic industries affected by AD/CV duty evasion. Some of these representatives stated that they had submitted allegations of evasion to CBP and expressed frustration that although they had requested updates from CBP on the outcomes of the allegations they submitted, CBP had not provided them with the information requested. CBP officials attributed this, in part, to the Trade Secrets Act, which they said restricts their ability to disclose the specific kinds of information requested. Additionally, CBP officials stated that they cannot disclose information about allegations involving active ICE investigations. Furthermore, CBP does not report on the results of its efforts at an aggregate level, which would avoid divulging restricted information while keeping key stakeholders informed. CBP officials stated that they are currently exploring ways to legally share what information they can on allegations with the parties that filed them.

Conclusions

Evasion of AD/CV duties undermines U.S. AD/CV duty laws—the intent of which is to level the economic playing field for U.S. industry—and deprives the U.S. government of revenues it is due. While CBP employs a variety of techniques to detect and deter such evasion, its efforts are significantly hampered by a number of factors primarily beyond its control. These include the inherently difficult and time-consuming process of uncovering evasive activity conducted through clandestine means, inconsistent access to foreign countries that limits CBP's ability (as well as ICE's) to gather necessary evidence, and the ease with which importers attempting to evade duties can change names and identification numbers to elude detection. Nonetheless, some improvements have been made since we last reported, including better communication between Commerce and CBP and CBP's encouragement of the use of higher bonding requirements to protect additional AD/CV duty revenue in instances where it suspects evasion. However, CBP lacks information from Commerce that it needs to better plan its workload and mitigate the impact of the time- and resource-intensive liquidation process on its efforts to address evasion. Further, CBP has no policy or mechanism for port officials to minimize the risk of port-shopping by notifying other ports about their use of higher bonding requirements. Unless these gaps in information sharing are closed, these recent initiatives may be compromised, thereby limiting the effectiveness of CBP's efforts to address AD/CV duty evasion.

CBP has also made some improvements in managing its efforts to address AD/CV duty evasion, including by developing better performance measures and monitoring its use of higher bonding requirements. However, it lacks key data on AD/CV duty evasion, including on confirmed cases of evasion and penalties, which could help it assess and improve its approach to addressing evasion and also inform agency and congressional decision makers about its efforts. Moreover, CBP has neither tracked nor reported the outcomes of the allegations of evasion it has received from third parties. Without improved tracking and reporting, agency leadership, Congress, and industry stakeholders will continue to have insufficient information with which to oversee and evaluate CBP's efforts.

Recommendations for Executive Action

To enhance CBP's efforts to address AD/CV duty evasion and facilitate oversight of these efforts, we make the following recommendations:

First, to help ensure that CBP receives the information it needs from Commerce to plan its workload and mitigate the impact of the liquidation process on its efforts to address evasion, the Secretary of Commerce should work with the Secretary of Homeland Security to identify opportunities for Commerce to

- regularly provide CBP advance notice on liquidation instructions, and

- notify CBP when courts reach decisions on AD/CV duty cases in litigation.

Second, to help minimize the risk of port-shopping by importers seeking to avoid higher bond requirements, the Secretary of Homeland Security should direct CBP to create a policy and a mechanism for information sharing among ports regarding the use of higher bond requirements.

Third, to inform CBP management and to enable congressional oversight, the Secretary of Homeland Security should ensure that CBP develop and implement a plan to systematically track and report on

- instances of AD/CV duty evasion and associated data—such as the duties assessed and collected, penalties assessed and collected, and the country of origin, product type, and method of evasion for each instance of evasion—and

- the results, such as enforcement outcomes, of allegations of evasion received from third parties.

Agency Comments and Our Evaluation

We provided a draft of this report to the Secretary of the Department of Homeland Security, the Secretary of Commerce, and the Secretary of the Treasury for their review and comment. We received technical comments from the Departments of Homeland Security, Commerce, and Treasury, which we incorporated where appropriate. We also received written comments from the Departments of Homeland Security and Commerce, which are reprinted in appendixes II and III, respectively. The Department of the Treasury did not provide written comments.

In commenting on a draft of this report, the Department of Homeland Security concurred with our recommendations addressed to the department that CBP (1) create a policy and a mechanism for information sharing among ports regarding the use of higher bond requirements and (2) develop and implement a plan to track and report systematically instances of AD/CV duty evasion and the results of CBP's enforcement actions.

The Department of Commerce generally concurred with the recommendation addressed to the department to work with CBP to identify opportunities for Commerce to (1) regularly provide CBP with advance notice of liquidation instructions and (2) notify CBP when courts reach decisions on AD/CV duty cases in litigation.

In its response, Commerce stated that both CBP and Commerce receive copies of injunctions from the U.S. Court of International Trade and attached a copy of a preliminary injunction to demonstrate how both agencies are generally served copies of the injunctions. However, when a court orders an injunction, such as the one Commerce provided, Commerce and CBP are enjoined[37] from issuing liquidation instructions or otherwise causing or permitting liquidation of the entries that are the

---

[37]Enjoin means to legally prohibit or restrain by injunction. Black's Law Dictionary (7th ed., 1999).

subject of the litigation. As a result, the injunction does not provide CBP with the information it needs to help with workload planning because it is not a court action that constitutes notice of the lifting of a suspension of liquidation, which would start the 6-month period in which CBP must liquidate entries. While an injunction can provide CBP information to help with workforce planning, it does not address CBP's concern for regular advance notice of forthcoming liquidation instructions. CBP needs information from Commerce on when final court decisions are reached to help enable the agency to better plan its workload and help mitigate the administrative burden it faces in processing AD/CV duties—an effort that diminishes the resources it has available to address evasion.

We are sending copies of this report to the appropriate congressional committees, the Departments of Homeland Security, Commerce, the Treasury, and other interested parties. In addition, the report is available at no charge on the GAO website at http://www.gao.gov.

If you or your staff members have any questions about this report, please contact me at (202) 512-4101 or gomezj@gao.gov. Contact points for our Offices of Congressional Relations and Public Affairs may be found on the last page of this report. GAO staff who made key contributions to this report are listed in appendix IV.

Alfredo Gomez
Acting Director, International Affairs and Trade

Appendix I: Objectives, Scope, and Methodology

To examine how the Department of Homeland Security's U.S. Customs and Border Protection (CBP) detects and deters the evasion of antidumping and countervailing (AD/CV) duties, we examined agency documents that outline CBP's process and methods for identifying evasion of AD/CV duties; reviewed laws and other documents that identify the enforcement options CBP uses to deter evasion; and analyzed data from CBP and U.S. Immigration and Customs Enforcement (ICE) on deterrence activities such as civil penalties, seizures, criminal arrests, indictments, and criminal convictions.

To identify factors that affect CBP's efforts to detect and deter AD/CV duty evasion, we examined CBP documents that highlight the challenges and the timeline associated with verifying evasion; analyzed data on the amount of civil penalties CBP has collected from importers evading AD/CV duties; and reviewed legislation governing CBP's use of seizures, internal memos on the use of single transaction bonds, and previous GAO reports on AD/CV duties.

To assess the extent to which CBP tracks and reports on its efforts to detect and deter AD/CV duty evasion, we reviewed CBP annual plans that identify its performance measures for addressing AD/CV duty evasion; documents that show CBP's performance against these measures; CBP testimony and videos publicizing successful efforts to address evasion; a CBP report to Congress on fiscal year 2010 efforts to enforce AD/CV duties; and a report by the Department of Homeland Security Inspector General on CBP's bonding process, including its use and tracking of single transaction bonds. Additionally, we analyzed data on civil penalties CBP has imposed for AD/CV evasion and allegations of evasion received from third parties.

Additionally, in the Washington, D.C., area, we discussed our objectives with officials in CBP's Offices of International Trade, Field Operations, and Intelligence and Investigative Liaison; ICE; and the Departments of Commerce and the Treasury, as well as a coalition of U.S. industries affected by AD/CV duty evasion.

To obtain a more in-depth understanding of U.S. efforts to detect and deter AD/CV duty evasion, we conducted fieldwork at the ports of Miami, FL; Seattle, WA; and Los Angeles, CA. We selected the port of Miami due, in part, to its proximity to CBP's National Targeting and Analysis Group (NTAG) for AD/CV duty issues; the port of Seattle due, in part, to the high number of civil penalties it imposed for AD/CV duty evasion over the last 5 years; and the port of Los Angeles because it processed the

most imports subject to AD/CV duties, by value, of any U.S. port. At each
port, we met with officials from CBP and ICE to discuss the efforts they
undertake to detect and deter AD/CV duty evasion at their port, the
challenges they face in detecting and deterring evasion, and the process
they use to track and report the results of these efforts. We also met with
representatives of the NTAG for AD/CV duty issues in Plantation, FL, to
discuss their methods for detecting evasion, both through their own
targeting efforts and through analyzing allegations of evasion they receive
from third parties.

To determine the reliability of the data we collected on AD/CV duty
orders, civil penalties, seizures, ICE enforcement outcomes (i.e., arrests,
indictments, and criminal convictions), and allegations received from third
parties, we compared and corroborated information from different
sources; checked the data for reasonableness and completeness; and
asked agency officials how the data are collected, tracked, and reviewed
for accuracy. Based on the checks we performed, our discussions with
agency officials, and the documentation the agencies provided to us, we
determined that the data we collected were sufficiently reliable for the
purposes of this engagement.

We conducted this performance audit from June 2011 to May 2012 in
accordance with generally accepted government auditing standards.
Those standards require that we plan and perform the audit to obtain
sufficient, appropriate evidence to provide a reasonable basis for our
findings and conclusions based on our audit objectives. We believe that
the evidence obtained provides a reasonable basis for our findings and
conclusions based on our audit objectives.

Appendix II: Comments from the Department of Homeland Security

. U.S. Department of Homeland Security
Washington, D.C. 20528

May 14, 2012

Alfredo Gomez
Acting Director, International Affairs and Trade
U.S. Government Accountability Office
441 G Street, NW
Washington. DC 20548

Re: Draft Report GAO-12-551, "ANTIDUMPING AND COUNTERVAILING DUTIES:
        Management Enhancements Needed to Improve Efforts to Detect and Deter Duty
        Evasion"

Dear Mr. Gomez,

Thank you for the opportunity to review and comment on this draft report. The U.S. Department
of Homeland Security (DHS) appreciates the U.S. Government Accountability Office's (GAO's)
work in planning and issuing this report.

The Department is pleased to note GAO's acknowledgement of the many external obstacles
facing the U.S. Customs and Border Protection (CBP) and U.S. Immigration and Customs
Enforcement (ICE) in enforcing antidumping and countervailing (AD/CV) duties evasion. The
report also appropriately recognizes that these obstacles are mostly beyond DHS control in
proving and determining evasion. In addition, we appreciate GAO's recognition that verifying
evasion of AD/CV duties is inherently difficult and time-consuming.

The draft report contained three recommendations designed to enhance CBP's efforts to address
AD/CV duty evasion and facilitate oversight of these efforts. The first recommendation was
addressed to the U.S. Department of Commerce and the second and third to DHS. Regarding
DHS, GAO recommended that the Secretary of Homeland Security:

Recommendation 2: Direct CBP to create a policy and a mechanism for information sharing
among ports regarding the use of higher bond requirements.

Response: Concur. CBP's Office of International Trade (OT) is including language in its
guidance to field personnel on the use of single transaction bonds (STBs) for AD/CV duty
evasion. This guidance will direct that field personnel request national targeting criteria (input
by the South Florida National Targeting Analysis Group) to alert officials at other ports when an
STB has been requested from an importer for suspected AD/CV duty evasion. Estimated
Completion Date (ECD): May 30, 2012.

Recommendation 3: Ensure that CBP develop and implement a plan to systematically track and report on:

- instances of AD/CV duty evasion and associated data—such as the duties assessed and collected, penalties assessed and collected, and the country of origin, product type, and method of evasion for each instance of evasion—and
- the results, such as enforcement outcomes, of allegations of evasion received from third parties.

Response: Concur. CBP's OT will continue to improve the Automated Commercial Environment's (ACE's) Validation Activity (VA) module which serves as the primary repository for information on AD/CV duty noncompliance. OT will develop the automated tools necessary to record this additional information and issue revised policy to field personnel requiring this information be entered into the VA module.

CBP's penalty data system, the Seized Asset Case Tracking System, is a case processing system and is not intended to track AD/CV duty evasion; rather, the ACE VA system tracks AD/CV duty and other trade noncompliance. In September 2009, CBP issued guidance to address data quality issues in several field offices, providing instructions to enter the specific missing country origin and commodity description or Harmonized Tariff Schedule classification related to penalties cited by the GAO. Additional guidance will be issued to field personnel this fiscal year re-emphasizing the importance of accurate data quality in penalty cases.

OT and the CBP Office of Field Operations will immediately begin to coordinate enforcement outcomes of allegations assigned to the ports. OT will continue to monitor the status of allegations assigned to the ports until such time that all enforcement avenues have been resolved. OT will keep allegations open until it receives a sufficient response from a port. Allegations will still be considered closed after their referral to Homeland Security Investigations/ICE because the analysis of the allegation is closed for CBP purposes.

To better inform the public on its efforts to detect and deter AD/CV duty evasion, CBP will also develop a plan and explore opportunities for reporting aggregate data on AD/CV duty evasion to the public. ECD: September 30, 2012.

Again, thank you for the opportunity to review and comment on this draft report. Technical comments for the report were previously provided under separate cover. Please feel free to contact me if you have any questions. We look forward to working with you on future Homeland Security issues.

Sincerely,

Jim H. Crumpacker
Director
Departmental GAO-OIG Liaison Office

2

Appendix III: Comments from the Department of Commerce

UNITED STATES DEPARTMENT OF COMMERCE
International Trade Administration
Washington, D.C. 20230

May 9, 2012

Dr. Loren Yager
Director, International Affairs and Trade
U.S. Government Accountability Office
441 G. Street, N.W.
Washington, DC 20548

Dear Dr. Yager:

Thank you for providing us with the draft report on Customs and Border Protection's (CBP) "Antidumping and Countervailing Duties, Management Enhancements Needed to Improve Efforts to Detect and Deter Duty Evasion" (Draft Report). We find the Draft Report both timely and helpful. We are submitting the attached technical comments in the hopes of clarifying some of the observations noted in the Draft Report. In conjunction with these technical comments, we are attaching a copy of an injunction issued by the U.S. Court of International Trade, including its corresponding service list demonstrating that both Commerce and CBP generally are served copies of Court injunctions. We stand ready to continue to work with CBP in enhancing and improving its efforts to detect and deter AD/CV duty evasion.

With respect to the U.S. Government Accountability Office's recommendations in the Draft Report, Commerce generally concurs with the first recommendation that the Secretaries of Commerce and Homeland Security work to identify opportunities for Commerce to (1) regularly provide CBP advance notice on liquidation instructions and (2) notify CBP when courts reach decisions on AD/CV duty cases in litigation. We note, however, that, in AD/CVD litigation, CBP cannot liquidate entries covered by an injunction until there is a final and conclusive court decision and Commerce cannot know whether any given court decision will become final and conclusive until all appeals are concluded or the period for all appeals has expired. Regarding the Draft Report's two other recommendations, Commerce has no comment other than to state that our agency is available to work with CBP to implement these recommendations should CBP seek Commerce's input and/or assistance.

We hope you find the technical comments to be helpful. We look forward to receiving the final version of the report. If you have any questions, please feel free to contact me at 202-482-5497.

Sincerely,

Christian Marsh
Deputy Assistant Secretary
for AD/CVD Operations

Attachments

Appendix IV: GAO Contact and Staff Acknowledgments

GAO Contact	Alfredo Gomez, (202) 512-4101, or gomezj@gao.gov
Staff Acknowledgments	In addition to the individual named above, Christine Broderick (Assistant Director), Aniruddha Dasgupta, Julia Jebo, Diahanna Post, Loren Yager, Ken Bombara, Debbie Chung, Martin De Alteriis, Etana Finkler, and Grace Lui made key contributions to this report. Joyce Evans, Jeremy Latimer, Alana Miller, Theresa Perkins, Jena Sinkfield, Sushmita Srikanth, Cynthia S. Taylor, and Brian Tremblay provided technical assistance.